AF472495

I am a Good Boy

Essential Life Lessons for Young Boys

Reuben Freeman

AuthorHouse™
1663 Liberty Drive
Bloomington, IN 47403
www.authorhouse.com
Phone: 1-800-839-8640

Published by AuthorHouse 3/6/2013

ISBN: 978-1-4817-2370-1 (sc)
ISBN: 978-1-4817-2371-8 (e)

Library of Congress Control Number: 2013903945

Table of Contents

"Respect At Home"

It is necessary, it is important, it is vital and it is respectful to show respect for your parents at all times.

Your grandparents are the parents of your parents, therefore they must be given the utmost respect.

You must always address your grandfather in this way, "yes grandpa" or "no grandpa," or by the name the family customarily calls grandpa or grandma.

You must always address your grandmother in this way, "yes, grandma" or "no grandma." – "good morning grandma" or "good afternoon grandma," you should never answer "yes" or "no," always use grandpa or grandma in your reply.

Your parents should be addressed in the same manner – "yes dad" or "no dad," "yes mom" or "no mom," or whatever the preferred name in your home is.

Always attempt to greet your grandparents, if they live with you, before you leave home in the morning. Always treat your grandparents with Honor.

Depending on their age and mobility, ask them before you leave home for school in the morning, if they need a glass of water, a glass of juice, the morning papers, the window shades open or closed, or an item from the store.

Your parents must receive the ultimate respect as well. Your parents have total responsibility for your health, welfare, and safety.

It is their responsibility, as your parents, to feed you, shelter you, protect you, and educate you.

In return, your responsibilities are as follows: -

1. Be respectful at all times, to your parents.
2. Be respectful to your teachers, at all times – you actually spend about one third of the day, five days a week, with your teachers – your teachers are responsible for you, while your parents are at work
3. Be respectful to your grandparents.
4. Be respectful to all elders in the home – brothers, sisters, uncles and aunts.
5. Go to school everyday – be on time for all classes.
6. Read – read – read – study – study – study.
7. Pass all tests or exams.
8. Always help your parents with tasks at home – make the bed – sweep the floor – mop the floor – wash the dishes – take out the garbage – separate the garbage in recyclable and non-recyclable – mixing of the garbage carries a fine, in certain cities and towns. Save that fine ,about $100 in some places, which can be used to buy something for the home, or to pay a bill.
9. Always be an excellent representative (represent) of your family – do nothing that would bring shame, ridicule, embarrassment, or disgrace on your family.

Be respectful of the Law – do not challenge the Law.

"Chores – Chores – Chores"

What is a chore? A chore is work in the house, and sometimes outside the home, that mom and dad normally do.

Actually it is their responsibility to get those things done. Chores are simple tasks such as sweeping – vacuuming – washing the dishes – taking out the garbage – sweeping the floor – sweeping the leaves from the sidewalk – washing your dirty clothes – making up the bed – changing the sheets.

None of these chores is "Woman's or Girl's Work." There is nothing embarrassing about washing the dishes, sweeping the floor, washing your clothes, or doing any chore in the home – this is responsibility.

It is unfair for mom and dad to return home, after travelling and a tiresome day at work, to see a sink full of dirty dishes, unswept floors, unmade beds, and a garbage can overflowing with garbage in the kitchen.

You must show appreciation for what your parents are doing, and the sacrifices they are making to provide the needs of the family.

It is not the respectful thing to do, when you allow your parents to return home from work, to wash dishes, take out garbage, sweep the floor, and prepare your dinner.

It is not girls work to help your parents around the house. Be a responsible son, by assisting your parents at home.

Make your parents proud and happy, when they return home, by helping with the chores.

Your parents may not be able to give you an allowance because of the bills they must pay every month – light bills – phone bills

– rent or mortgage – car payments – your cell phone bill – and other expenses.

You can help your parents save money, if they are the owners of the house you live in.

All homeowners, by law, must keep their sidewalks clean – free of garbage.

Every homeowner, must put the garbage, on the sidewalk, on the appropriate day, to be picked up by the Sanitation Department.

IN certain cities and towns, the garbage must be in the right containers, and must be separated in recyclable, and non-recyclable.

All garbage, especially from the kitchen, must be covered to prevent dogs, cats, and rats from feeding on the garbage.

Rat infestation can occur if garbage with unwanted food is placed in an open can, in your yard or on the sidewalk. Cover the garbage and save the fines.

In the winter season, homeowners are also responsible for keeping the sidewalk directly in front of their homes, free of snow and ice.

Why are they responsible for keeping the sidewalk free of snow and ice? It is the Law.

If a pedestrian slips and falls, on the snow or ice, and hurts himself as a result of that fall – fractured foot, or a broken hand or rib, or any other injury, the homeowner can be sued by that person for pain and suffering, medical bills and possible loss of income, as a result of falling on the ice or snow on the sidewalk, in front of that house.

Your parents can suffer tremendous financial losses, if such an incident should happen because you did not assist in removing the snow and ice from the sidewalk – your parents must pay the penalty as ordered by the Court.

"Keep Your Family Informed Of Your Whereabouts At All Times"

"Always tell a family member where you are going, before you leave home."

It is very important that mom, dad, grandma, grandpa, brother, or sister, know where you are at any time of the day or night. You can also leave a note, or a message on their phones. Why is this important? If there is a family emergency, or a natural disaster such as a hurricane, flood, or earthquake, your family will know where to find you.

If there is an allegation against you, your parents, or other family member can be your alibi – they can verify that you were at a different location than the one where the alleged incident occurred.

An "alibi" is a confirmation, proof, or witness to an event in time and place. For example, if you were accused of stealing a pair of sneakers at 5:00 P.M. on a certain day, at a certain time, but you were at the dentist on that same day, at the same time, then your "alibi" is your visit to the dentist, and the dentist himself.

Always tell someone where you are going – parents who want to know where their children are, are not "Helicopter Parents" – they are loving parents, concerned parents, who care about the safety of their children.

"You Must Respect Your Peers"

You must respect one another, in school, and out of school – on the basketball court – on the football or baseball or soccer field – on the block – at a party – at the mall – at the movies – or any other place – always show respect for one another.

If you step on someone's toes, or accidentally walk into a person, male or female, you must say to that person, "Excuse me," or "I am sorry."

If someone steps on your toes, or accidentally walks into you, and he or she does not acknowledge it by saying, "I am sorry," or "Excuse me," you must take two steps backward. Do not step toward that person – this is confrontational or threatening behavior.

It is unwise to fight because someone stepped on your toes or accidentally walked into you – knives, guns, fists, or any kind of weapon can get you or the other person, or an innocent bystander seriously hurt – paralyzed – in jail – or killed .It is not wise, or smart, to start a fight, because someone, accidentally or not, stepped on your toes and/or Nikes sneaker.

Respect one another – accidents do happen – you lose nothing if you just walk away – and you would have saved yourself from a serious injury, or you would have saved your life.

It is a good thing to greet one another, as is the custom in our society, and many other societies, with the appropriate greeting of the day – "Good morning" or "Good afternoon" – "Good morning Richard" or "Good afternoon Mary."

If you do not know the name of the person, if the person is a female, say "Good morning Ms."

Never greet a female in the following manner – "Hi Bitch" or "what's up Ho." – this behavior shows a total lack of respect for all females.

If the person you are about to greet is a Senior Citizen or Elder, and whose name you do not know, greet him in this manner – "Good morning Sir" or "Good morning Maam," if a female.

You disrespect your friends, and fellow students, when you disrupt the class – you also disrespect the teacher, anytime you disrupt the class.

"Give Respect To All Teachers"

Every teacher, whether or not, he or she teaches you, must be respected, at all times.

Do you know that every Professional in this world has a teacher. Teachers are the foundation of the world.

Take a look at why all teachers must be respected –

The President of the most powerful country in the whole world, the United States of America, had a teacher.

Your parents had a teacher – some of you have parents who go to school at nights.

Your teacher had a teacher.

Your dentist had a teacher.

The bus driver had a teacher.

Your pastor had a teacher.

The man who founded McDonald's had a teacher.

Your sports heroes such as Michael Jordan, Venus Williams, Tiger Woods, LeBron James, and all others, had teachers.

Your parents have jobs to earn money needed to provide for the needs of the family – food, clothes, rent or mortgage, electricity and other needs.

If your parents should disrespect their supervisors or bosses, at work, they would be fired, and lose the ability to provide money for the needs of the family.

You have a job also – a student, a full-time student.

Your boss is your teacher, and your teacher is your boss.

Your teacher has the authority to tell you what to do, and what not to do, whenever you are in his or her classroom.

Your paycheck is a High School Diploma, and a College Degree.

You will not receive these paychecks, unless you complete the job. That job is for you to complete all courses.

The completion of all courses, satisfactory completion, is required to earn a High School Diploma and a College degree.

Every job has a job description – what you have to do to complete the job and get paid.

Your job description is as follows –

1. Attend classes everyday.
2. Be on time everyday.
3. Be attentive in class – do not interrupt the teacher while she is teaching.
4. Study – study – study.
5. Read – read- read.
6. Always respect your teachers.
7. Pass all your tests.
8. Complete all class projects.
9. Respect all staff members.
10. Respect all school rules.
11. Last, but not the least, respect yourself.

"Respect School Property"

What is school property?

1. The students' desk and chairs
2. The teachers' desk and chairs.
3. The blackboard, chalk, and eraser.
4. All posters on the classroom walls – do not deface them or tear them down.
5. All interior walls, including the bathroom, and lunchroom – no graffiti or writing on the walls.
6. Textbooks and all other books in the classroom, to include magazines and newspapers.

Your parents pay a percentage of their incomes – income tax- to pay for services available to every family member.

These services are – police protection – education (schools) – fire services – sanitation services – ambulance services – health and hospital services, and many other services.

For example, if your mom or dad, earn $400.00 every week as a Postal Employee, the income taxes taken out of her paycheck of $400.00 might be approximately $133.00. This is called a Deduction. Portions of the Deductions go to the City, State, and Federal governments to pay for services mentioned above. Her take home pay is now $267.00. Therefore if you are destroying school property, you are destroying property your parents' taxes paid for.

"Respect A Person's Opinion"

One person may see a color as blue, while another person may see the same color as black.

We see things from different points of view, because of our age, experiences, education, cultural background, upbringing, religious beliefs, and other reasons.

Do not readily dismiss another person's opinion. Everyone is entitled to his or her opinion.

It is good to listen to another point of view or opinion.

A coin has three sides – front – back – the edge – some coins have smooth edges, while others have rough edges.

We can learn from others – life itself is a school. We can learn, and do learn something new everyday, based on what we see, hear, or read.

Therefore, it is important to listen. We must listen to what is said. Let the other person complete his or her thoughts. Do not shout them down.

Another person's opinion is not wrong because his or her opinion is the opposite of yours, or not the same as yours, on a particular topic.

Neither is your opinion wrong, because it is not in agreement with the other person's opinion.

"Always Show Respect For Women (Females)"

All females – your mother – grandmother – sisters – cousins – aunts - the Librarian – your teachers – the school safety officer – the school crossing guard – the Police Officer – your female class or schoolmates – females at your church, and all females with whom you come in contact with.

All females should be respected – young and old – fat or thin – females of all races – females of all nationalities – females of all religions – short or tall females – rich females and poor females – women of all hues and colors.

You should address females whose names you do not know as" Ms." You can also address these as "Maam."

Open a door for a female – hold the door open until she gets in or out. Open a car door for her, to get in or out of the car. Offer her the front seat of the car, if you are travelling with her.

Offer, or give up your seat to a female, when she boards the train or bus.

Give up your seat to a Pregnant Woman.

Help a female with an obvious heavy package she may be carrying or trying to lift.

Offer a female, the appropriate greeting of the day – "Good morning Ms." or "Good afternoon Ms. Elizabeth."

Never use foul language in the presence of females. Do not have lewd conversations in the presence of females, never call a female "a bitch," – never call a female a "whore"– never refer to a female as a'' prostitute" – this is disrespectful behavior – it is not right – it is wrong. Do not touch or fondle a female, any female, especially a stranger.

Do not pull a female by the hair – play or no play. Never hit a woman, regardless of what she may have said or done to you, or did not say or do – assaulting a woman (female) physically can get you arrested.

Such behavior also shows a lack of respect for the woman, and a lack of respect for yourself.

Do not ask a young lady for sex, especially someone you do not know – this is known as sexual harassment, as is fondling and touching and feeling of body parts, such as her buttocks. A sexual harassment allegation or charge is a very serious matter. You can be arrested if a female complains to a Police Officer that you indecently touched her.

If a young lady, refuses to talk to you, walk away from her – do not verbally abuse her – do not call her a "Ho" or a "Bitch." She has the constitutional right to refuse your sexual advances, or attempts to have a conversation with her.

Do you want to be known as, in legal terms, a sexual predator, sexual deviant, or a sexual molester.

Anyone of these labels, if attached to your name, will have a devastating impact on your life, for a long time to come.

One of the consequences, may require you to move out of the neighborhood, and leave behind your friends and family, because of your sexual behavior.They may have to leave the neighborhood with you, because they are responsible for you.Most people do not want to have a sexual deviant, molester, or predator, living anywhere in their neighborhood.

What would you do, if a female member of your family, is sexually harassed or molested.

If you as a juvenile, is convicted of committing certain sex crimes, your name will be entered on a special registry, known as the "Sex Offender Registry." If you fail to perform the requirements of the registry, you can be labeled "a felon."

Your name can remain on the Sex Offender Registry for as long as 20 years to life.

"Respect Other People's Property"

It can be very costly to you and your parents, if you steal, damage, or deface other people's property.

Here are a few examples –

1. Do not steal a fellow student's coat, sweater, cell phone, or cash.
2. Do not sit on, scratch, break a window, steal the hub-cap, or cause any other damage to anyone's car parked on the street, or in a driveway.
3. Do not throw rocks or bottles at windows – cars, buses, or homes. If caught, you and your parents can be taken to Court, and ordered by a Judge to pay a fine.
4. Do not throw candy wrappers, soda can or bottles, straws, used facial tissues, used paper napkins, sandwich wrappers, or other kinds of garbage on someone's lawn, or in their flower garden.
5. Do not destroy, or pick the flowers in ones garden, as you pass by.
6. Other people's property include any item in a store, bodega, supermarket, clothing store, shoe store, candy store, or any business in a shopping mall.

No exchange of cash for anything you take will get you arrested.

"Do Not Take What Does Not Belong To You"

Never take what does not belong to you – do not even take it home – to take what does not belong to you is called "stealing." To steal anything is considered a "Criminal Act."

It is not "fun" to steal – if you are caught stealing, or with stolen goods in your possession, you will be arrested, taken to the police precinct in handcuffs, and ordered to appear in Court before a Judge, who will impose a penalty on you, for stealing.

The penalty can vary – probation – restitution – fines – community service – jail time – or whatever penalty is appropriate to fit the crime you are charged with.

The act of stealing – a criminal act – can be very costly to your parents – the cost of bail – the fines imposed by a Judge – hundreds of dollars to retain an attorney to represent you in a cCourt of Law – the cost of replacing the item you stole, if so ordered by the judge – and maybe, pay lost at work, because your parents had to take time off from work to accompany you to court, time for which they could not be paid.

Would it not benefit the family, to spend hundreds of dollars to pay the rent or mortgage, the light bill, your cell phone bill, grocery bill, and other bills, instead of spending hundreds of dollars on Attorney's fees, bail, restitution, because you broke the law, disrespected your parents, and disrespected the person whose belongings you stole.

These hundreds of dollars could have been saved for your college tuition.

It is unwise to steal anything, for example, a pair of sneakers, because your friends are wearing one. Ask your parents to buy it for you, or save your allowance to buy one. Your parents may not have the money to buy that sneaker for you, but this is not a reason to steal what you want, but does not need.

If you are caught stealing, your parents will have to spend hundreds of dollars more than the cost of the item you stole – think about it – does it make sense to steal anything – even the theft of a pack of gum, or a single candy, is a criminal act.

Criminal activities will put you in prison for a long time. Is this the lifestyle you want – in and out of prison?

Felony convictions can cause you to lose many benefits, which law abiding citizens are entitled to – the right to vote , gainful employment opportunities – certain benefits or services – funds for education (financial aid), and the privilege of serving your country in the Armed Forces.

Respect your parents – Respect the Law- Obey the Law –

- Always –

"You Must Have Respect For Time"

Everyone in the world has the same amount of time – 24 hours each day of the week.

You may have heard someone say "I don't have enough time." How can that be, when each of us, has 24 hours each day of the year.

The absence of "enough time is dependent on how one uses time.

Time must be managed carefully, everyday.

Write down every activity for each day. For example, the amount of time spent in school – time spent in the Library – time spent traveling between home, school, and the Library.

By looking at how much time you spend doing these activities, you may need to change the order in which you do these things. Maybe you could go to the Library immediately after you leave school, instead of going home, and then go to the library, or spend less time in the Library.

The monitoring of the use of time is called "time management." Another example of time management, is to monitor the number of hours you sleep everyday. Instead of going to bed at 8:00 P.M., you can go to bed at 10:00 P.M. instead, and use the extra two (2) hours to read, write an essay, or solve a math problem.

On the other hand, you can go to bed at 8:00 P.M., and awake at 4:00 A.M. in stead of 6:00 A.M. and still have two (2) hours to read, write, and solve the math problem. Therefore you cannot use the excuse ,"I don't have enough time," if you continue to go to bed at 8:00 P.M. and arise at 6:00 A.M. to prepare for school.

Some people are habitually late, and blame everything and everyone for their lateness.

They blame the weather, they blame the bus, they blame the traffic, they blame their dog and cat for their lateness – they never blame themselves – they do not practice time management.

The people who get a lot done in a day, plan how to use each day – every hour of every day is accounted for in a written plan – this is time management.

You should get to bed on time, and wake up on time – you should catch the bus on time or the train on time. Use the train or bus schedule to assist in your travel plans. Keep a copy of the schedule in your backpack or book bag, and on the wall somewhere in the house.

You should always arrive, on time, at school.

You should arrive at church, on time.

You should arrive, on time, for all appointments, for example, the dentist, or the doctor.

You must show up, on time, for your summer job interview.

You should be home, on time, for the family dinner.

You should always be on time.

Time is money – Money is time.

"You should always be on time for school"

In order to arrive at school on time, you need to prepare for school the night before.

Here is what you should do –

1. Complete your homework before you go to bed.
2. Pack your bag with the books you need for that day – pens – pencils – pencil sharpener – eraser – rulers – your completed homework – any notes for your teacher, and other items you need for classes that day.
3. If you do not wear a school uniform, select the clothes you will wear and iron them, if necessary.
4. If you wear a school uniform, prepare it before you go to bed – iron the uniform, and c lean your shoes, polish and shine your shoes.
5. Go to bed early on school nights – you should suspend watching TV, playing video/games, long phone conversations, or face book activities.
   Use the time for studying. The more you study, the better you will do on your tests – your grades will improve.
   Reading is essential. You should read at least 2-3 books a month. Read – read – read. You must have a library card, and use that card often – read – read – read.
6. Get up on time – use an alarm – set the alarm to repeat at least 15 minutes after the time it was set to alarm – hit the snooze button.
   For example, if you want to get out of bed at 6:00 A.M., you set the alarm for 5:30 A.M.., and the repeat alarm for every 15 minutes (snooze time). You now have 15 minutes to half an hour of extra sleep, and two more wake-up calls.
7. Secure your bus pass, ticket, metro card or tap card, or cash, to get on the bus on time.
8. You should leave home at least fifteen (15) minutes to thirty

(30) minutes earlier, to arrive at school on time – this extra time compensates for delays, such as slow traffic, accidents, or Police activities, or bad weather.

For example, if it takes one hour to get to school, and you normally leave home at 7:00 A.M. , leave home at 6:30 A.M. or 6:45 A.M.

9. If you do not have the fare or bus pass to get on the bus, do not enter the bus by way of the back door – this is illegal – it is fare evasion – you can be arrested.

   Tell the driver you do not have your pass or card, and politely ask him to allow you to board the bus. In most cases, the driver will give you permission to board the bus.

   You must acknowledge his kindness with a "Thank You."

   The driver is in charge of the bus – show him respect, show her respect. The driver can be the friend you need, if at another time you don't have the bus pass.

"Why Is It Important To Be on Time For Classes"

In life, time is very important.

The sun or moon does not show up late in the skies.

If this should ever happen, the earth can be devastated by disorder in the seasons, lack of rain, too much rain, floods, hurricanes, damage to our food crops, or no growth of food, and many other natural occurrences that can destroy our way of life.

It is also said in the Business World that "Time is money, and Money is time."

What happens when you arrive late for class?

1. The teacher is interrupted, and the class is interrupted.
2. Your fellow students are distracted.
3. One or more students could miss the information, or parts of it, that the teacher was imparting.
4. The teacher may, if time allows, be forced to revisit that topic or subject.
5. Just as important, you have missed out on valuable information, because you were late.

   The classroom is the training ground for you to take your place in society.

   Punctuality is required of you in the workplace, just as it is in the classroom.

   You must stop making excuses, and blaming people or things for your lateness.

   Be responsible, do not blame the bus.

   Be responsible, do not blame the rain.

   Be responsible, do not blame the traffic.

   Be responsible, do not blame the alarm clock.

   Be responsible, do not blame the dog.

   It is solely your responsibility to do what you should do to get to school on time.

You must be aware of the fact that school is preparing you to take your place in society as a teacher, school principal, President of the United States, a carpenter, plummer, policeman or fireman or astronaut, or whatever you chose to be in life – be responsible – be responsible – be responsible.

"Silence In The Library"

The Library is a place for reading, researching, studying. It is a place for learning – respect the Library and everyone who uses it.

You must respect the Librarians, the security officers, and all other employees of the Library, with whom you deal, when you are using the Library.

The Library is not a place for phone conversations – put your phone on silent or vibrate, when you are in the Library.

The Library is not a place to hang out.

The Library is not a place for loud conversations.

The Library is not a place for obnoxious, loud conversations, laced with expletives.

The Library is not a place to steal personal belongings.

The Library is a huge reservoir of knowledge.

You can learn a whole lot about the world in which you live. You can learn a whole lot about people, places, animals, space, the sun and moon, the rivers and oceans, mountains, trains and planes, the food you eat, and the water you drink, the chicken and beef you eat, your ancestry, and so much more.

Information on the career you choose, can be found on the bookshelves in the Library – do not depend only on what you learn in school, or what the teachers teach you.

Go to the Library and learn more, and more, and more – the more you know, the better it is for you.

If you have nothing to do, do not do it in the Library. Show respect for the Librarian, staff, students, grandfathers and grandmothers, and all others who use the Library, because they are eager to learn.

Do not deface the books or magazines, or any other Library material – all information must be preserved and cared for, so that those who want to learn can have access to all of the information they seek.

"Do Not Play In The Classroom"

The classroom is your place of business – the classroom is your office.

The classroom is also the place of business and office, of each of your classmates.

The business you have in the classroom is the business of learning.

The teacher is your coach – your teacher is training you to be a Professional in whatever profession you choose. Your teacher is preparing you to take your place in Society.

What you learn in the classroom, is absolutely essential for the time when you assume certain responsibilities in Society.

The teacher is your boss, and your boss is your teacher. Your teacher is authorized to tell you what to do – your teacher is authorized to tell you what not to do – he or she has the authority to dictate to you, what is acceptable in the classroom, and what is not.

You must give respect to all teachers, as you will be expected to give respect to your supervisor or boss, when you get your first job.

When you play in the classroom, while the teacher is teaching ,you are disrespecting both the teacher, and your fellow students.

A teacher gets paid the same amount of money every pay-day, whether or not you want to learn.

You are hurting your fellow students, and yourself, because some of the information the teacher gave out is missed, or not understood, because you interrupted the class, the teacher may not have the time to visit that particular lesson again.

When your disruptive and disrespectful behavior forces the principal to summon your parents for a conference, you embarrass your parents, and make them take time off from work, to meet with the school authorities, time off for which they may not be paid.

"Be Honest – Do Not Cheat On Your Test"

You must be honest – dishonesty can hurt you – you can lose the trust of your parents, brothers, sisters, your teacher, or anyone you associate with, if you lie, cheat, or steal.

Dishonesty can cause you to fail your tests, and miss earning your High School Diploma.

Dishonesty can get your expelled from school or College – dishonesty can make you lose your job – dishonesty can lead to an arrest and time in prison.

To avoid cheating on your tests (dishonesty), it is wise to attend all classes, on time, daily, and be attentive in class. Whenever you interrupt the class by arriving late, talking as the teacher is teaching, or acting as the class comedian or clown, you deprive both yourself and fellow classmates of the information the teacher is imparting.

The loss of information on any subject can be the difference between passing a test and failing a test. Do not be afraid, or feel ashamed or embarrassed, to say to your teacher, "Miss Jones, I do not understand how to solve this problem, please explain it to me, thank you." You should always ask your teacher, or a classmate to assist you with any subject or topic with which you are having difficulty.

If you leave those difficult questions unanswered, you may very well fail the next test, because those questions can appear on the next test, or questions on the next test can be based on those questions you failed or did not understand in the previous test.

You should always seek immediate help with a subject, a math problem, a history or science idea, you did not understand in class. Never leave what you do not understand for tomorrow. Seek an explanation now. If you do not know the meaning of a word, look it up, in the dictionary now, so that you can understand the context in which it is used, not as a separate word, but as it is used in the whole sentence, or paragraph.

To avoid the need to cheat, you must do the following –

1. Study regularly – read a lot – to read and understand what you read is extremely important.
   Every subject requires reading – history – math – geography – chemistry – music – basketball – football – and all other subjects of interests.
2. Respect the teacher - pay attention in class.
3. Do all class projects.
4. Do all class work.
5. Do all homework.
6. Get to class on time everyday.
7. Attend all classes everyday.
8. Always seek help on all subject matters you do not understand.
9. If you failed a test, ask your teacher to explain to you what you did wrong, and how to arrive at the correct answer.

A cheater, obviously, does not have the information he or she needs. You can acquire the information if you work to attain it. The only work you need to do is "study – study – study – study – study – study and study."

"Do Not Take Gifts From Strangers"

The gifts can be any or a combination of the following – candy, ice-cream – a car ride – money – a toy, or a Game Boy – a pair of sneakers, tickets to a basketball game – a meal at McDonald's or Burger King – and many others.

Why you should not take gifts from strangers? There are men and women, who encourage, or entice, young boys and girls, to engage in criminal activities, such as stealing, sale of drugs, transportation and distribution of drugs, use of drugs, lookout for drug dealers, break into cars, steal cars, snatching jewelry, snatching women's pocketbooks, stealing men's wallets, stealing credit cards, and the very latest, snatching people's I-phones.

If you snatch someone's phone with the intention of using it – do not do it – the owner will report it, and the phone company, Apple, Samsung, AT&T, or whichever dealer sold the phone will turn the services off – you cannot use it

It is not smart to steal an item, that is of no use to you, or cannot use, and go to jail for it. Is that smart?

When in prison you will lose your independence – you will be told everyday when to go to sleep, when to eat, when to take a shower, when to turn the lights out – do you want to live like this?

Some of these people who offer gifts to children can be very dangerous people, even killers.

They kidnap boys and girls, and take them far away from home, and seriously hurt, or kill them. These kidnapped boys and girls may be found days, weeks, or months later, or may never be found alive again.

There are also people who kidnap other people's children, because they do not have children of their own.

There are people known as child molesters, or sexual predators or sexual deviants – they kidnap young boys and girls, and take them away to their homes, or a hideout, or secret place, to have sex with them, or use them as prostitutes.

These children are locked away for a long time, from their families, and are sexually abused, and may even be killed.

There is another group of people who love to have sex with children only.

They pay a person who is involved in "child prostitution" to bring young boys and girls to them for sex. These young boys and girls are never paid – all the money goes to the man or woman who kidnapped them.

These young boys and girls are physically abused, sexually abused, raped, sodomized, brutally beaten, and some may be killed.

Do not take anything from strangers – run away and shout for help, if a stranger offers you money or anything else. Go home and tell your parents. Tell your teacher, if you were on your way to school – tell a policeman, or the school crossing guard – run into a store, shout for help, and say what happened to you.

Do not keep what the stranger did a SECRET. You must tell your parents. Tell a policeman if one is near – protect yourself and other children – tell someone immediately – not tomorrow – tell someone as soon as possible.

And last but not least, and very, very important, you should never go into the car, or truck, or SUV of a stranger.

There are evil people, who drive around looking for boys and girls.

They ask the boys and girls for directions,offer them a ride home, or snatch them and drive away with them. These boys and girls are actually abused, and sometimes killed.

Stay away from strangers who call you ,or offer a ride, or ask for directions.

Run away and tell a policeman, or a school crossing guard or the shopkeeper, or your teacher. Tell someone as soon as possible. By all means, call your parents immediately, if a phone is available.

"Criminal Activities – The Possible Costs To Your Family"

Our society has Rules and Regulations each of us must observe.

These Rules and Regulations provide for an Orderly Society.

Anyone who violates these Rules are expected to pay a Penalty or Debt.

The penalty or debt can be any or a combination of the following – restitution– community service – fines – imprisonment, ranging from days to weeks, or months to years, or life imprisonment or death.(execution).

You must obey the Law – these Laws are for the safety of members of the society, and to prevent acts that are offensive and harmful to society.

You are a member of the society – your parents are members of the society – your brother is a member of the society – your sister is a member of the society – all your relatives and family members are members of the society.

The following violations are among the most frequently committed by young men, and in some instances by young women as well – public urination – loitering – littering – jumping the turnstile (fare evasion) – jumping out of the taxi without paying the fare (fare evasion and theft of of service) – shoplifting – stealing (even a stick of gum) - spitting on public transportation – defacing public property (graffiti) - loud music on public transportation – bus or subway -robbery - assaulting someone - bullying - assaulting a teacher -

smoking marijuana, or the use of illegal drugs - weapons possession, and other violations of the Law.

You will be caught if you continue to break the Law – it may take one day, one week, one month, one year or ten years, but you will be caught if you continue to break the Law.

You will be penalized when caught, to the fullest extent of the Law.

Surveillance cameras are in many places in the community, recording and watching people's activities.

Any fines or other forms of penalty imposed on you by a Court of Law, because you had violated the Law, will definitely have an impact on your parents' paychecks.

Do you know what your mom's or dad's salary (paycheck) is?

Maybe not – let's assume your mom's salary is $1400.00 bi-weekly.

Would she bring home the whole amount of $1400.00 – No, she cannot bring home the whole salary. . .

Why not? Have you ever heard of taxes? Every employee must pay a percentage of their salaries to the government as taxes.

There are three government bodies, that require every employee to pay a certain amount of their salaries as taxes, depending on how much they earn, and how many persons they have to support.

For example, your mom has to take care of you and your brother and sister, therefore she has four dependants, including herself.

Therefore she is a taxpayer with four dependants, and pays taxes based on her claim of four dependants, and the amount of money she earns.

"Why do Employees pay taxes?"

The money paid from an employee's salary, as taxes, to the government, Federal, State, or City, is used to provide the many services we receive as citizens

These services include police protection – fire protection – ambulance services – health and hospital services – air traffic control – bus and subway services – schools – daycare – senior citizens centers – parks – sanitation – school crossing guards – life guards on the beaches, and at the pools in the summertime, and many more services.

A percentage of the taxes goes to pay the salaries of the service providers such as the policeman and schoolteacher.

The following scenario describes how your parents pay check would be affected, if you violate a law –

A notice on the train reads, "NO littering: violation of this law brings a penalty of a $200 fine."

But you ignored the warning, and dropped an empty soda can, and a cheeseburger wrapper on the seat.

A policeman on the train is one of the many witnesses to your violation of the law.

He gives you an appearance ticket to appear in Court and pay the $200 fine.

You cannot pay the fine – you are a student – you do not have $200 – you have no job.

Who pays the fine? – your parents pay the fine, because they are responsible for you.

But your mom pays taxes from every paycheck, to subsidize the trains and buses she uses to get to work daily.

The $200 fine is more than what your mom would pay for a month's ride on the subway. Even more directly, the $200 fine is more than the subway fare for one month, for example, the unlimited fare for one week in New York City is $29.00 each week or $116 each month - the monthly fare is about $104.00. This $200 fine could be used to buy food, pay a phone bill or put into a savings for future college tuition.

Take a look at another hypothetical violation of the law which has several consequences for your whole family.

Let's assume you, and four of your friends, went to the mall not to buy anything, but to hang out.

One of them pilfers a baseball cap from a store shelf, and slips it into his backpack.

He then proceeds to leave the store without paying for the baseball cap, but is intercepted by the security guard, because the anti-theft devise on the cap, triggered an alarm. He is searched, the baseball cap is found in the backpack, and all five of you are arrested, because you were judged to be accomplices, as you were seen, as a group, walking through the store.

Your parents now have to retain an attorney to defend you in a Court of Law, and prove you innocent in this matter.

The cost of retaining an attorney can be hundreds of dollars and could be thousands more, depending on the severity of the offense.

One or both of your parents will have to take time from work, to accompany you to Court, and may not be paid for the time spent in Court.

Your parents may have to pay twice, or three times the cost of the property stolen for the following reasons (1) restitution of the property stolen may be ordered by the Judge (2) hundreds of dollars to retain an attorney to represent you in Court(3) possible loss in pay for the time spent in court with you.

Does your mom or dad have hundreds or even thousands of dollars to retain an attorney to represent you in Court. Could your parents afford to take money from their savings or other accounts – money they need to pay the rent – pay the mortgage – buy groceries – make car payments – pay the light bill – pay the gas bill – pay your cell phone bill – or future college tuition.

Think about it – is it wise to break the Law!!

You should ask your parents to show you the bills they have to pay each month.

You should learn all you can now – how parents take care of their families, because in the near future you will also have a family.

"Always Respect Police Officers"

To become a Police Officer, one must attend the Police Academy where a police recruit receives intensive training in Law Enforcement.

At graduation, each Officer takes the Oath of Office, which stipulates that each Officer will protect and defend the citizens in the town, village, city or county, and state in which he or she is employed. The Officer must uphold the Laws of the country as well.

Every Officer is authorized, to arrest and bring the appropriate charges, against anyone who is caught breaking the Law.

In some states, the seemingly simple act of crossing the street against the red light can get you a summons for "jay-walking."

The Officers uniform, which includes a badge, that identifies him or her as a Police Officer, are symbols of the authority he or she has been given to uphold the Law, and make arrests.

The Police Officer must also protect himself while protecting the public.

There are persons who do not like Police Officers and would readily harm any Officer who stands between them and any criminal act they are about to commit. For example, the robbery of an individual, or a business place.

A criminal can be very dangerous, and a threat to the Officer's life, if he knows he is about to be arrested, and would therefore do whatever he thinks he should do to get away.

Therefore it is necessary to communicate with any Police Officer, in the right and respectable manner.

If you are stopped by a Police Officer, you must comply with the orders or commands you receive.

You should address the Officer by the name on his badge. If you cannot see or read the badge, address the Officer as "Yes Sir," or No Sir" or "Yes Maam" or "No Maam,"

As a result of the criminal's need to avoid arrest, he will try to hurt the Officer in any way possible, for example, with a knife, or other sharp object, hitting with the intent of seriously hurting the Officer, and the worst of all, shooting the Officer, which can lead to death and serious injury of the officer, or an innocent bystander.

When you are asked for your identification, you must say, "Officer, my I.D. is in my pocket" before putting your hands in your pocket to retrieve it. "Officer Johnson," my I.D. is in my backpack," before you open your backpack to retrieve the I.D. If your I.D. is in your wallet, take it out and give it to the Police Officer.

Always tell the Officer where your I.D. is before you make any attempt to pull it out.

On too many occasions, wallets and cell phones have allegedly been mistaken for weapons, especially guns. Because of this situation , innocent citizens were shot by police officers, and either seriously wounded or killed.

Never try to run, whether or not you did something wrong, when a Police Officer gives you an order to stop.

Stop immediately – stop immediately – stop immediately – keep your hands at your sides or wherever your hands are when you receive the order to "stop."

When you get the order to "stop," do just that. Do not move even a finger.

If your hands are in your pocket, keep them there, and wait for further instructions from the Police Officer.

Do not try to take out your wallet or cell phone. Do not anticipate what the officer will do. Wait for his orders.

If the officer is behind you, when he or she gives you the order to "stop," you must stop immediately with your hands wherever they are when you stop. Do not turn around – do not move – turn around, only when the Police Officer tells you to turn around – you must turn around slowly with your hands wherever they were when you received the order to "stop."

Put your hands wherever the Police Officer tells you to put them. Carefully follow his orders.

Police Officers must always protect themselves by using the procedures they were taught at the Police Academy.

"Homework – Homework – Homework"

Do you like homework? Do you do your homework?

Do you know that homework is very important? Yes homework is very important.

Why is homework important? Well, homework is practice – it is like basketball, or football, or baseball.

A Professional or non-professional, goes to the court everyday to "shoot hoops." He or she shoots hoops everyday, to improve their skills at throwing a basketball, through the hoop.

Everyday on the basketball court, shooting hoops, increases the number of times the ball will fall through the hoop – practice makes perfect. Shooting hoops daily will increase your accuracy.

Michael Jordan and LeBron James are great basketball players, simply because they practice, and practice, and practice, everyday on the basketball court.

To be successful at earning your High School Diploma and College Degree, you must have the same attitude, or work ethic, as a Michael Jordan or LeBron James – practice – practice – practice.

Hit the books – read – read- read – do your homework – complete your homework – ask for homework.

Homework reinforces the work you do in class. Homework makes you a better student.

Homework enables your teacher to know how strong or weak you are in a particular subject, for example, history, or math, and can use this information to give you additional assistance to improve your performance in those subject areas.

As a result, your grades will improve – you can go from a “C” grade to an “A” grade or a “B” grade.

Homework is also an opportunity for you to get additional help from, mom, dad, or a brother or sister.

You should always do your Homework.

"Hygiene – A Clean Body – Head To Toe"

There are several organs in our bodies, such as the heart, which pumps blood throughout the body, but the largest organ is actually the skin.

The skin covers you from head to toe – it is the skin which removes perspiration or sweat from the body.

The body sheds skin continuously. Shed skin, which is dead skin, mixed with perspiration (sweat) is really bad smelling (malodorous).

A shower or bath removes the dead skin and perspiration which dried on your body. A shower is usually a refreshing experience, either hot or cold.

Some people sweat profusely, even with little physical activity.

Others sweat after a run, walk, a game of basketball, football, tennis, a climb up or down a stairway, a bicycle ride, or any activity that requires the use of your hands and or feet, in a laborious way.

The season of the year, or weather conditions, also control the amount of perspiration you put out – the hotter the weather, the more sweat you are likely to put out.

It is good hygiene to take a shower early in the morning, and before you go to bed at night, especially after a ballgame.

You must not wear today, the clothes you wore yesterday, unless they were washed the night before.

A build-up of two (2) days of sweat and shed (dead) skin will emit a foul and offensive odor.

Your underwear – T-shirts – briefs – boxers – must be changed daily, and washed before they are worn again. Your hair should be washed every time you take a bath or shower, especially in hot weather – perspiration or sweat comes out of the top of your head, and is lodged in your hair along with dead skin.

Your feet should be properly washed also – the bottom of your feet and between your toes. Foot powders are recommended. Your socks must be washed also.

The appropriate underarm deodorant should be used after a bath or shower, and a body powder or a cologne, with a mild fragrance. Use cologne sparingly - do not pour or spray it on profusely, or in excess over your body. Too much cologne on a man's body can be intrusive and offensive.

Dental hygiene is also important – brush daily – brush after each meal, if possible. Brush your teeth before you go to bed at nights – do not sleep with food particles – beef – chicken – shrimp – cheese – or any other food particle stuck between your teeth, or in your mouth – you should visit your dentist regularly.

"Always Go To School Prepared For Every Class"

You must always get to school prepared, and on time.

1. Before you leave home, be certain you have your bus pass, ticket, metro card, or cash to get on the bus or train.
2. Pack all your tools or instruments in the backpack or bag, on the night before – pens – pencils – erasers – rulers – textbooks, notebooks – dictionary – geometry kit, and other items required for that day in class.
3. Completed homework.
4. Completed class projects – science – history – math, etc., turn in all projects on time.
5. Signed documents your teacher needs from your parents.
6. Questions for your teacher, about anything you do not understand in your homework assignment, or about the work you did in a prior class.
7. You must have at least two (2) pens that write.
8. You must have three (3) sharpened pencils when you leave home. Your pencils should not be shorter than four (4) inches – carry a pencil sharpener with you – always.
9. The edges of your ruler must be smooth from end to end, on both edges – you cannot draw a straight line, if there are indentations or cracks on the edges of the ruler. All markings on the ruler must be visible.

“How Should I Behave In Public”

You are the representative (you represent) of your family, whenever you are away form home – at school – at church – at the movies – at the bazaar – at the mall – on the bus – on the train – at a party – at McDonald’s – at a game – at the supermarket, or anyplace in the community.

You are expected to obey the Rules of Society, such as –

1. Pay the fare on the bus or train.
2. Do not enter a taxi, if you have no money.
3. Pay for every item you pick up in a store, before walking to the exit, even if it is a stick of gum.
4. When shopping, use the basket or cart to put the items in, and take them to the check-out counter, or cashier.
5. Do not put your feet on the seat, when on the bus, or train.
6. Do not jostle fellow passengers, especially the elderly.
7. If you step on someone’s toes, say, “I am sorry” or “Excuse me.” Be respectful.
8. Do not snatch ladies’ handbags – it is not a game, it is a crime.
9. Always carry identification when you leave home. Do not leave home without it. Turn back, go home, and get it, if you don’t have it on you.
10. Do not get into arguments with strangers.
11. Whenever you have an appointment at the doctor’s office, the dentist or the ophthalmologist, or anywhere else, you should sign the visitor’s logbook.

It is important, not only for the doctor, it is especially important for you .Your signature in that logbook, is called an Alibi. Your Alibi.

An Alibi is a confirmation, or witness to where you were and what you were doing, and who you were with at a certain time of a particular day, month and year.

For example, if someone should accuse you of stealing a pocketbook, on the same day, and at the same time you were in the doctor's office, then your alibi – your signature in the visitor's logbook in that doctor's office, is proof that you did not do what you are accused of.

Many students go to the shopping mall or a business strip, after school to socialize or "hangout."

A few may buy a cheeseburger and a soda, and sit and eat their meals, while engaged in conversation.

Others congregate on the sidewalk, sometimes blocking pedestrian traffic, and behaving in a disorderly manner, that triggeres the intervention of the stores security personnel, or in more serious situations, Police Officers.

There is nothing wrong with meeting friends at the mall, as long as these gatherings are orderly, and considerate of the business owners, and their prospective customers, who ply the sidewalks on their way to make purchases. It is inconsiderate to block the sidewalk and entrances to business places.

Some customers are scared off by the presence of scores of young people, standing around the entrances of stores they want to enter.

As a result, they go to other stores where the entrances are not blocked, and make their purchases. A business does lose money, if the entrance is blocked.

The food court is another place where students frequent. The food court is a place to eat, therefore it should be treated as the dining room in your home.

The tables at the food court are not seats. No one should sit on a table – tables are for plates, cups, glasses, knives, spoons, and forks, and food.

Do not put your feet on the chairs – chairs are for sitting. They are not footrests.

The beds on display at the mall, are not there for frolicking – stay off the beds.

You must respect the storeowners property.

Loud, obnoxious, and disorderly behavior, can be intimidating to certain members of the public, especially in confined or closed spaces.

Women with babies and toddlers, will leave for fear that their children might be in some form of danger.

Senior Citizens can feel unsafe in the presence of such behavior, and will also leave the store – a loss for that business.

It is advisable to leave an area where the behavior of persons is threatening and intimidating.

Public disorder or disorderly behavior can get you arrested.

If arrested, your parents may have to use their limited financial resources, to retain an attorney to represent you in a Court of Law. They may have to borrow. The costs can be hundreds of dollars.

Can your parents afford to pay an attorney, or pay fines ordered by a Judge, because you made a decision to challenge and disrespect the Laws of Society, and also disrespect your parents.

A criminal record can damage your prospects for employment, housing, social services, your right to vote (in most states), and even acceptance in a college.

If you are designated as a felon, by the Judicial System, you may be disqualified from receiving financial aid for college expenses.

Respect others, be polite to others, respect people's property, and public property – bus shelters , the interior and exterior walls of the buses and trains, no spray painting or etching – the walls of your school building. These are only a few examples.

Obey the Laws of Society. Respect yourself. Respect your family whenever you are away from home, You are the representative of every member of your family. Do nothing to bring shame and embarrassment on your family.

"Prepare For Life"

As a young man, you are given the opportunity to "Prepare for living," or life, as the process is known.

This opportunity, is available to you, through the efforts and sacrifices of your parents, who are doing their utmost to take you to that moment in your life, when you assume complete responsibility for yourself.

One of the happiest moments in the life of any parent, is to attend their child's college graduation ceremony. It is a great accomplishment for that son or daughter, and the parents as well – a truly joyous moment in ones life, a proud moment.

To get to this point in life, requires preparations on the part of both child and parents.

What is preparation? Preparation is to set up, put together, create or build.

What did your parents do to prepare – obviously they were disciplined at home and at school.

They went to school on time, most of the time, if not all of the time, whether it was rain or shine, did all their homework, and class projects, studied hard, and passed their tests, which earned them a High School Diploma and a College Degree. Some parents take two buses, or train and a bus, or one long bus or train ride to get to work.

When they return home after an eight-hour workday, and two or three hours of travelling, they prepare dinner, wash dishes, take care of a younger brother or sister, prepare your clothes and hers, for the next day, and supervise home-work.

This is a full day – There are also moms and dads, who go to school after work, and arrive home late at night.

All parents need the assistance of their children who are old enough, to do chores, such as sweep, mop, wash dishes, take out the garbage, and even wash clothes, either at home or the laundromat.

Dad's assistance is also needed. Mom should never be left to do all the work by herself.

Every son, must help perform chores at home.

Boys must help to wash dishes, sweep the floor, vacuum the floor, mop the floor, wash the clothes, and more.

There is nothing effeminate, about helping mom and dad at home. Helping at home is not "girls' work."

You must be of help to your wife, when you start your family – help out at home now, while learning to take care of your future home.

Your parents, your elder brother or elder sister, are the most important and most visible role models in your life.

They prepare you, or groom you, in many ways, to assure your place in society.

They taught you to speak, read, write, dress, how to use money, how to travel to the corner store and beyond, to respect others, how to behave both at home and in the public, maybe, how to fry an egg or boil an egg, and how to tell time.

Your mother is at the top of the list, because it is believed that a child begins to learn in its mother's womb, before it is born.

Your parents, on a daily basis, rise early, prepare for work, leave home early to be on time, regardless of the weather.

Sometimes they need to work longer hours, or overtime, to earn extra money, for items the family needs.

The definition of the word prepare is – set up, put together, create or build.

You must be prepared for whatever it is you have to do, to go wherever it is you want to go, and achieve your goals in life.

If you have to wake up, at 5 o'clock in the morning, to take a shower before leaving for school, you must be awake at 5:00 A.M. on your own, by an alarm, or by a family member. Then you must take to the bathroom, soap or shower gel, toothbrush and toothpaste, shampoo if needed, and your towel.

You are not prepared for your shower, when you turn on the water, and discover that the soap or shower gel is missing, (if these items are not stored in the bathroom).

Now you have to turn off the shower, dry some of the water off your body, put on your pants, or wrap yourself in your towel, and leave the bathroom to get the shower gel.

This lack of preparation results in your losing time, and arriving late at school.

As a result of your lateness, you missed a whole class period, and the information your teacher passed out.

The loss of that information can, and may affect your performance on the next test, or on one of the major examinations, for example, the SAT.

School is an important part of your preparation for the years ahead of you – your life.

As you grow older, you will start to gradually assume the responsibilities your parents now have for you.

At the age of eighteen, society proclaims you to be an adult. What does that mean? It means that you are now responsible for yourself and your actions, and decisions you make from day to day, for the rest of your life.

You are now free, as an adult, to make decisions without the help or approval of your parents – they don't have to sign any documents any more – you sign for yourself – you are an adult.

Moral responsibilities, legal responsibilities, financial responsibilities, and other responsibilities are now yours.

A good education is essential for living (life)

You are taught in school to solve mathematical problems, spell, read, write, think and make decisions, or come to conclusions, based on the information available to you.

What you learn in school equips you to function in life – out in the community – the supermarket – the restaurant – the doctors office – travel – communication with strangers – read and understand purchase contracts, for example, a car, a cell phone or a house, your employment agreement or contract, and many more.

You eventually, will make important decisions, confidently, without advice or consent of your parents, with certain exceptions such as buying a home, or major decisions such as getting married.

Many transactions involve a written agreement, between buyer and seller, or provider and receiver of a service, that explains what is expected of each party in the agreement, according to the product sold or service provided.

The signature of each party in the agreement, is required on the written agreement, to say that the agreement is now in force.

Any side which violates or fails to follow what was agreed to can be taken to Court, for failure to honor his part of the signed document.

The benefits you earn at school is not only the ability to read, write, and do mathematical calculation, you also learn to be punctual, follow instructions, make decisions based on the information you receive, as in comprehension, learn a foreign language, teamwork, communication with persons of different backgrounds, and many other skills, that will come in handy in the society where you complete your college Degree, and enter the workforce.

The IMPORTANCE of discipline in ones life."

What is discipline? Discipline is training, grooming, preparation, self-control, self command, and self restraint.

A disciplined student is a student who does what is necessary for him or her to be a success.

Those necessary things are – punctuality, near perfect attendance, completion of all homework assignments, completion of all class projects, be attentive in class, be respectful of all teachers, ask questions, study frequently at home or at the library, read, read, read, spending less time watching TV, or playing video games, always seeking teacher's help with a math, science, history, or any other subject which he or she does not fully understand.

If you failed to give the right answer to a test question, always ask the teacher to explain that question to you – never leave it unanswered, because that same question, could appear on another test.

The disciplined student has a sense of direction.

He or she knows what the goals are, therefore that student does all that is required to achieve those goals.

When a student disrespects his teacher, fellow students, or anyone else, he or she automatically disrespects himself or herself.

Some of the witnesses to your despicable behavior, will say, "He has no training," or "He is just like his dad," or

" He has no parents."

Many negative comments are made about your mom or dad, or both ,when your behavior is inappropriate, and most of the comments come from persons who do not know who your parents are.

It is embarrassing for your parents when they are asked to meet with your teacher or principal to discuss your inappropriate behavior.

Your respect for your parents, must be extended beyond home and to the classroom, and everywhere else in society – at church- at the movies – on the bus – on the train – in the clothing store-at the mall – at the basketball game or court.

Your inappropriate and anti-social behavior can have negative consequences for your parents and you, or the whole family.

Your teachers lose nothing, when you interrupt the class, arrive late, miss class, refuse to do homework, and class projects, and show nothing but disrespect for them.

Their pay is not reduced or confiscated when you engage in conduct, in the classroom, that shows a lack of respect for them, and the students who want to learn.

Our society has many rules which are also known as Laws, Regulations, Procedures, and Protocols which are simply guides to how things should be done.

These rules provide for safety, order, continuity and uniformity. They prevent confusion and doubt about how things are done.

Communication is made easy.

Communication involves not only speech, but it is a common acceptance that there are certain ways in which things are expected to be done (common law).

For example, stoplights, and stop signs, provide for a free flow of traffic – ignore the traffic lights and stop signs, and nothing but chaos and destruction of life, limb, and property happens.

Without establishing rules the world would be a dangerous place to live.

Society demands discipline from home to school to the workplace – to the shopping mall – to the movies – to the ballpark – to the supermarket, and many, many, other places.

School plays a major role in preparing you for your future years. – Life as it is called.

As you grow older, you will gradually assume, the responsibilities your parents now have for you.

Many teenagers are anxious to receive their work permits, but "work permits" come with serious responsibilities, hence the reasons to take school seriously, and do all that is required of you, and more, to earn your High School Diploma, and College Degree.

School is an important part of the process of preparing you to take your place in society.

The training and discipline you receive in school is carried over into Society.

As you are required to be on time for classes, study, do class assignments study and pass your tests to receive a diploma, and show respect for your teachers, so it is at your future place of employment. You will be required to show up for work, on time, every day, do exactly what you are hired to do and respect your supervisors.

Do otherwise, and you will be made to pay a penalty – probation – loss of pay – suspension, or loss of your job, depending on the Rules and Regulations of the job.

Discipline is grooming – your parents and teachers are grooming you, or preparing you to take your place in society.

You are being groomed to replace one of many professionals who are fast approaching the age of retirement,age 60 to 65, and in some cases beyond the age of sixty five years.

Depending on your choice of Profession, you will be replacing the President – a teacher – policeman – doctor – U.S. or State Senator – the Mayor – Congressman – fireman – nurse – school principal – auto-mechanic – electricians – soldier – gynecologist – airline pilot – sanitation worker – postal employee – dentist – traffic agent, or one of many other professionals.

In addition to qualification (discipline), you must have workplace discipline.

What is workplace discipline? Workplace discipline is not very different from school discipline.

You must be punctual – on time everyday, and do not exceed the time allotted for lunch or coffee brakes – follow all instructions or directives from your supervisor – do not use work time for personal business – do not use your employees phones or computers for personal business.

Any job, part-time or full-time, carries responsibilities with which your employer trusts you.

Those responsibilities are for the successful operation of your employer's business.

The end game is to make money – if you fail to carry out those responsibilities, you will be fired.

No employer will keep an employee who is causing his business to lose money.

It is also a loss of money to the organization when an employee is inefficient – it costs money to train an employee – so if that employee is late, lazy, does not complete tasks, and habitually absent, and takes more time for lunch breaks, than is allowed, he or she will eventually be fired.

An employer will not employ anyone who is weak in reading, writing, and mathematics, where these skills are required. If any of these deficiencies appear on your job application, resumé, or during the interview, you will not be hired.

Every workplace has guidelines, for performing whatever duties are assigned to its employees, depending on the job – pilot – policeman – teacher – chauffeur – and others. These guidelines have different names – Rules, - Regulations-Protocols-Instruction Manual

A Safety Manual is one of the most important Guidelines every employee should be familiar with.

Your safety, the safety of your co-workers, safety of the building and other occupants, is of extreme importance.

Certain businesses must have licenses to operate.

If they are found to be operating without the appropriate license or permit, from the government agency that oversees or regulates that business, the owners can be forced to close the business, until the appropriate license or permit is issued.

The regulating government agency – City, State, or Federal agency, each has its own Rules and Regulations for a particular business operation.

Some businesses do fall under the jurisdiction of one or more of the three government agencies.

These Agencies are empowered to close temporarily, or permanently, any business which is found in violation of the Rules and Regulations under which they are allowed to operate.

Instead of closing, fines and other punitive measures are used to penalize those businesses that violate the laws.

"It Is OK to Speak Well"

There is nothing wrong or embarrassing about speaking well, in life. There is an appropriate time and place for everything. even speaking well.

Can you wear your beach clothes in church? No, it would not be appropriate.

Can you play games on your phone during classes? Of course, not. Such behavior will not be tolerated – there is a penalty for that sort of behavior.

Therefore, street language is not appropriate for the classroom, place of employment, business place, or transaction of business, negotiations of a sports contract, or a contract to buy a home.

The classroom is the place where all students are taught to spell, read, and write well, and also speak well.

A good command of the English language is essential for communication with other persons in the society, outside of your circle of friends where street language is often used, and the business world, from your school to Wall Street.

The official language of the United States of America is the English language. A businessman, from a foreign country, who does not speak English is provided an interpreter to make it easy for him to transact his business.

In other countries, the official language varies from country to country. In France, the official language is French, in Brazil the official language is Portuguese, and in Germany, the official language is German.

All of your school records are written in English, not street languages.

Cell phones and I-phone contracts are written in English,as well as other languages.

Your ability to function well in Society, and to protect you and your family's interests requires you and your family to read, write, and speak well.

"It Is Important To Dress Appropriately"

School prepares you to take your place in society. You will be taking the place of one of several professionals depending on what profession you choose.

You could be filling the place of the President of the United States of America, a U.S. Senator, a Congressman, a City Council person, a teacher, a doctor, a policeman, an attorney, a carpenter, an auto mechanic, an electrician, a sanitation worker, or one of many others.

In addition to academics, you also learn the following –

1. Time management.
2. Respect for authorities.
3. Respect for others (fellow students).
4. Respect for the organization you represent (your school).
5. How to dress appropriately.
6. Teamwork (classmates, teachers, and teammates (sports).
7. Leadership (class president, student body president, others).

Do rags, gang colors, pants with huge holes in them, loud music – from your cell phones in class or in the hallways, pants worn ,to expose your underwear, below the butt. This style of dress is not appropriate for school.

Some schools requires a uniform – the same dress code for every student in the school. For example, blue shirt, navy blue tie, black pants, and black shoes.

If your school does not have a uniform, thereby all means, be tidy, wear clean clothes and that includes your briefs, boxers, and T-shirts. Your shoes and socks should be clean also. If you wear leather shoes, clean and shine them regularly.

You should always wear a belt on your pants. The belt should be fastened on your waist. Your pants must be on your waist and above your underwear, brief or boxer shorts.

You are improperly dressed, if your underwear is exposed and your pants is sitting just below your buttocks,, or on your knees, as if you are about to sit on a toilet seat.

As viewed from the front. Your pants should not be below, or on your genitals, which appears as a huge bulge. This is vulgar, and disrespectful behavior.

It is inappropriate to dress in this manner, as many young men do, when they go for job interviews.

You will not be hired, if you appear for an interview dressed in this manner. There is a time and place for everything, and that includes the way in which you dress.

When you join the workforce, you will be expected to dress according to your employer's dress code.

"The Three Modes of Dress"

1. The Formal.
2. The Informal or Semiformal.
3. The Casual Dress.

Each mode of dress is a dress code for special occasions or places. The Formal dress, is the appropriate wear for occasions such as the office, weddings, dining at certain restaurants, and theater, a job interview, a salesman, a doorman, an usher at church, and many others. The formal dress, the suit, included a dress shirt, which can be white, blue, a striped shirt, or other color of choice, a jacket and matching pants, and black or brown shoes polished to a shine.

The Tuxedo is an elegant Formal Dress.

Pin-striped suits can also be worn – some men wear hats as part of the Formal wear.

The host of an event may request a particular color of suit be worn, for example, a wedding, 18th birthday, or sweet sixteen party. When a specific dress code is stipulated for an event, always follow the code.

Most Up-scale restaurants require a complete suit as the mode of dress for dining.

You will not be admitted if the dress code is not followed. Save your date and yourself the embarrassment of being turned away because you are not appropriately dressed.

Sneakers and jeans are not part of the Formal or Informal wear, neither is a do-rag.

The business suit can be either a solid black or solid navy blue suit.

The Informal or Semi-formal wear is a suit minus the jacket, or a suit without the tie. A turtleneck can be worn, instead of a shirt and tie.

A sport coat can be worn with or without a tie.

Informal affairs can include birthday parties, graduation parties, a nightclub or just a simple house party.

Always pay attention to the mode of dress required for an event, and dress accordingly.

The pants must be worn on the hips at all times, supported by a belt. Your underwear must never be exposed.

The “Casual dress” does not require a suit.

The Casual dress can include sneakers and jeans, sandals, polos, short or long pants, cap or hat, and any colors you choose.

Casual dress is not appropriate for a job interview, unless it is so stated.

Too many young men, and women, show up for interviews dressed improperly, or inappropriately.

Your prospective employer is not interested in the color, or brand, or style of your underwear.

Your prospective employer is interested only in your resumé, which will indicate whether or not you can be an asset to his business. Can you help his business make money – your underwear cannot and will not.

Your prospective employer also uses your unwritten resumé to decide whether or not he will hire you – yes, y our unwritten resumé. Your unwritten resumé is your appearance. First impression counts – first impressions are very important.

An appropriately dressed and well-groomed applicant is the first impression an employer gets, when that applicant walks into his office for the very first time to apply for that job.

Your appearance may be the deciding factor as to whether or not you are hired.

Your appearance can get you fired before you are hired.

"Tools For School"

Your school is, your workplace – your job title is,STUDENT. You will receive two major paychecks – a High School Diploma and a College degree.

You will earn two big paychecks because you would have completed all that was required of you at your workplace (school).

But you cannot be successful at your job, unless you have the tools required for the job – you must use all the tools necessary to do an efficient job.

The tools you need are as follows: -

1. Pens – you should have at least two (2) pens, because one may fail to write.
2. Pencils – you should have at least three (3) pencils, and a pencil sharpener. Each pencil must bed sharpened before you leave home. If one pencil point breaks, you will have to more to work with – no time lost.
3. A ruler – the ruler must be in working condition. Its edges must be smooth, so that you can draw a straight line.
4. A dictionary – it is important for you to know what a word means (definition) as you are reading – not hours or days later.
5. All required textbooks for every subject.
6. Geometry instruments and other instruments necessary for chemistry and other classes.
7. A Library card – why? – There are many books about the subjects you are studying in school. Therefore you should

go to the Library and get more information on what you are taught in school.
The more you read, the better you will be at writing and comprehension and the wider your knowledge will be.You will also see an improvement in your grades.

8. Separate notebooks for each subject.

-Always be Ready-

"The Importance of Learning" (Education)

All schools, from kindergarten to college, prepare their students for life, which includes the workplace.

You are required to attend school everyday, be on time for each class, respect all teachers, do what the teachers ask you to do, study, do your homework, complete all class assignments, dress appropriately, and last but not least, pass your exams.

Those requirements are the same for the workplace .

The employer pays his employees x number of dollars per hour for an eight hour day, five days a week, to perform certain tasks.

Therefore the employee is expected to arrive on time everyday, to perform those tasks. Each task is a responsibility the employer has entrusted to his employee, for the successful operation of his business.

If you fail at the responsibilities entrusted to you, the employer will fire you.

The employer will not tolerate any actions that causes him to lose money, or the trust of his business partners, and, clients, or customers.

If you are paid to work eight hours a day, you are expected to arrive on time, each day, and work for eight hours.

Any loss of money to the employer you incur, is actually a portion of the wages he pays his employees. Therefore to prevent these losses, the employee must say, "You are fired."

When you graduate from college, and enter the workplace, you will be subject to a dress code.

You may be required to wear a uniform or another dress code. For example, white shirt, black pants, red tie, and black shoes, or dress pants, no jeans and sneakers.

Many uniforms identify the employee with the organization he or she works for, a few examples are, the Postal Service, UPS, the Army, the Fire Department.

You are the representative of the Corporation you work for. You are the face of that Corporation.

Therefore you must conduct business with the customers and clients in a professional manner, and always according to the Protocols of the Corporation.

You are expected to be polite, respectful, considerate, attentive and caring. You should always say “Thank you,” to the customer or client, at the end of the transaction.

Your interaction with clients or customers, must never bring ridicule or embarrassment to your employer – such attitudes can cause your employer to lose clients which results in loss of money to the business.

On a daily basis, many students across this country, who are excelling in class by earning A’s and B’s on their exams, are called names such as nerd, bookworm, dweed, or bore, and in some cases are physically abused.

It is wrong to verbally or physically abuse these students – they are preparing for the future – you are not.

Your favorite football or basketball player – your favorite athlete, must do the work necessary to remain on the team, or be fired.

The professional athlete, must be on time everyday for practice. He must be present for team meetings – he must be present for scheduled interviews with the media– he must complete his medical check-ups – he must be on time to travel with teammates on the team bus or plane to the next game.

All personal activities must be done on his time off – visits with family members or friends – parties – movies, and other activities. There are no excuses for doing otherwise.

You as a student, should follow the same work ethic as the

professional athlete. If your ambition is to become a professional athlete, then school is an important part of your preparation to become not only an athlete, but to be whatever you want to be – an athlete – a doctor – a pilot – a fireman – the President of your country – a Policeman – an electrician – an auto mechanic, or whatever you choose to be.

Anyone who signs a multi-million dollar contract, or works a regular 9-5 job, is subject to the same rules of the workplace – both employees work for a boss, and both can be fired, if they do not follow the rules.

The rules are the same for all students – attend school everyday – be on time everyday – do all homework – complete all class assignments – respect your teachers – follow all school rules.

Your paycheck is your diploma – you will not get paid if you do not follow the rules.

Most of the "A" and "B" performing students who are teased, ridiculed, called names, and verbally and physically abused, makes sacrifices, and follow the same work ethic, as the professional athlete.

They show up for classes everyday – so can you, and so should you.

They arrive for classes everyday, on time – so can you and so should you.

They do their home-work and all class assignments – so can you, and so should you.

They study everyday – so can you, and so should you.

They watch little or no TV during the school weak – so can you, and so should you.

They do not play video games when they should be studying – so can you, and so should you.

They visit the library regularly, and read, and read and read – so can you, and so should you.

They do not waste time on face book- so can you, and so should you.

We all have the same amount of time each day – 24 hours – do not waste time – use time in a productive way – study – study – study – do your homework – read, read, read.

You must always work to earn A's and B's.

You must never take the advice of any teacher who tells you that a "C" is O.K.

It is never OK just to work for a "C" – always reach for the highest star – the "A".

You may not get there sometimes, but at least you are still high in the skies with "B's. and "C'".

"D's" are down on the ground – this is not where you should be.

"F's" are flat on the ground, or your back – this is never the position you want to be in, where everyone is stepping all over you.

Always aim for the highest in achievement – the "A's."

"It Is Good To Be A Volunteer – Community Service"

What does it mean to "volunteer" – Perform a service for someone, or group of people ,without the benefit of pay or any form of compensation.

A volunteer can also join any branch of the military – Army, Air Force, Navy, Marines, the Coast Guard, or National Guard, without being ordered by the government to do so, as in a draft. When one volunteers to serve in the military, he or she does receive a paycheck.

In case of a severe threat to the security of our country, the government may find it necessary to order young men and women to serve in the military.

Volunteering can be advantageous to you, if you are considering certain Professions as a career.

For example, if you want to be a nurse, or doctor, you should volunteer to work in a hospital or a nursing home, or if you want to join the Police Department, you should join the Police Department's Explorer Club.

There are many opportunities in your community for volunteers. Start with your church – find out from your pastor who needs help. There are Senior Citizens, members of your church, who need assistance in grocery shopping, or in going to the bank, at certain times of the month.

Other opportunities for volunteering are –

1. Volunteer to tutor fellow students, or a child in church, or on your block, who needs help with math, English, or any other subject.
2. Volunteer to move snow from your elderly neighbor's steps and sidewalk.
3. Volunteer to assist a blind person cross the street.
4. Volunteer to help clean the neighborhood park – be a leader, form a team with your buddies and take them to clean the park.
5. Volunteer to help at a Veteran's Hospital (V.A.).

The patients in a V.A. hospital, or Veteran's hospital, are the men and women, who as soldiers, took up arms to defend their country, against foreign enemies, for example, the "911 attack" on our country.

These patients suffered many physical injuries from mild to severe, and among them are those who were hurt psychologically.

There are patients in V.A. hospitals who receive few or no visits from relatives or friends, because of death, distance from the hospital, lack of interest, and other reasons.

You can play games with them, watch movies together, have conversations with them, assist them at mealtime, and engage in many other activities such as field trips.

This is a great way of honoring these men and women, who gave bravely and unselfishly, their services in defense of this country.

Volunteer activities enhance your college application.

"Start Working On Your Goals Now"

It is not too early to start preparing for your career now – pilot – doctor – mechanic – nurse – teacher, or whatever Profession you choose.

Reading and comprehension are essential skills for learning and mastering any subject.

So, if you want to be a pilot, for example, go to the Library and read up on such related topics as the weather, geography, stars, jet engines, and of course, what pilots do.

Do not wait until high school or college to learn about pilots and airplanes.

Your reading should also include other topics.

There are a lot of amazing things in this world.

The earth is a very tiny part of the universe – a grain of sand in comparison.

There are volcanoes and earthquakes, tsunamis and monsoons.

There are mountains under the oceans, and rings of fire under the ocean.

There are birds and fishes, dolphins and whales.

There are different peoples – Chinese and Japanese, Africans and Russians, Native Americans, and Eskimos.

The more you read, the more proficient you will be in reading and comprehension.

This skill makes it easier for you to study any subject successfully – your grades will be excellent.

Do not wait until you start college to begin learning about your chosen profession.

Be ahead of the game, start now at whatever level you are in Elementary or High school, 4th grade or 6th grade, 9th grade or 12^{12} grade – start your preparation now.

Investigate internet sites, such as -

1. Live Science.com
2. NASA.T.V.
3. National Geographic
4. Discovery Channel

Always check your TV Guide for educational programs.

"Speak To The Professionals In Your Field Of Interest"

If you have already decided what your career will be, then it will be a good idea for you to speak to someone who is doing exactly what you want to do.

Do you want to be a fireman? Speak to a fireman. Ask him to tell you what he had to do to wear a fireman's uniform. For example, a fireman's job is physically demanding, then you will need to prepare by joining a gym for physical training.

Do you want to be an auto mechanic? Introduce yourself to your neighborhood mechanic. Tell him you want to be an auto-mechanic, and would like to volunteer to work with him after school, so that you can be a few steps ahead of the game, when you start college.

You should also go to the Library and borrow books about auto mechanics.

Do not wait until you enter college to start learning about auto mechanics – help yourself – start now – read now, about your chosen profession – when you get to college you will be prepared for those classes in auto mechanics.

Do you want to be the President of the United States of America? Write a letter to your Congressman or Senator, and a letter to the President. Tell them of your ambition.

Seek out a person who does what you want to do, and ask him or her to be your mentor.

"Role Models"

The role models of most boys are professional athletes, such as Michael Jordan, LeBron James, Koby Bryant, Derrick Jeter, and others.

You see these role models only a few times a year,on TV,when they are playing their respective sports.

When the sports season is over, you do not see them or hear about them until the next season.

The role models you see everyday are your parents, an elder brother or sister, your neighbor, your teacher, the Postal Employee who delivers your mail every single day, rain, snow, or shine, and many other role models.

These are people, like many others, good citizens, who rise every morning, and leave home early to get to work on time, to earn money to provide the needs of their families.

One person may earn more than the other, but they still go to work everyday, regardless of the weather, to meet their families' needs, food – clothing – rent mortgage – light – gas – cell phone bills, which includes your cell phone – college tuition – and many other obligations.

Your parents are your most obvious role models – you see them go to work everyday, and may hear them talk, from time to time, how stressful their workplace is, how disrespectful their boss or supervisor is, or how jealous or envious their co-workers are because they received a good compliment, or a Certificate of Achievement from their supervisor, because of their excellent work performance.

You may have to face similar work conditions, when you enter the workplace. Talk to your parents, or any of the role models mentioned above, about their jobs, so you can learn from them, how to manage certain situations you may encounter when you start to work. This is one way of preparing yourself to become an employee.

"It Is O.K. To Sit Properly"

Yes it is appropriate to sit properly, at all times, regardless of where you are, even at home.

Rules (or customs) of Society must be observed.

Violations of rules can result in your paying a penalty, or receiving some form of punishment.

The penalty can range from mild to severe – from a fine to jail time, depending on the severity of the violation.

It is not proper behavior to sit with your feet on a chair, especially with your shoes on – shoes pick up dust, dirt, oil, feces, dog feces, bird droppings, tar, and other material, that would fall off the soles of your shoes, unto the chair.

The person who sits on the chair you just had your feet on, will pick up any of the above mentioned items, on his or her pants, or dress, or on their skin, if a short pants is worn.

Chairs are for sitting – chairs are not footrests.

The same applies to seats in the classroom, on the bus, on the train, seats at the bus stop, seats at the mall, or seats in the park, and at home. It is rude and inconsiderate to put your feet on the back of a chair, when you are at the movies.

You must not sit with your legs sprawled, or wide open when traveling on the bus, train, or subway. The seats must be shared with fellow passengers. This is a violation of the Law, and you will be penalized if caught.

Passengers have paid for the seat you have your feet on.

"Preparing For A Job Interview"

Preparation is essential for everything you do in life. If you do not have a ticket to get on the train, you cannot get to where you want to go.

Employment is a necessity of life for most people, therefore you must be prepared for the interview.

Time is important – Time is Money, and Money is Time.

Before starting out for the interview, you must know the location of the office, and how to get there. You should not be calling the office to find out how to get there, on the day of the interview.

You should leave home at least an hour earlier than the estimated start out time, so that you can arrive on time for the interview – this extra time gives you a cushion in case of traffic delays, bad weather, road emergencies, and other incidents that might increase your travel time, which would cause you to arrive late for the interview.

If you are delayed by heavy traffic, or a bus or train delay, you must call the office as soon as possible to notify them of the delay, and possible late arrival. Do not want until you arrive at the office, and say, "I am sorry for being late, traffic was heavy." Always call ahead of time, and notify your potential employer of your travel situation.

If you cannot show up for the interview, because of an emergency call the office, as early as possible, and ask to reschedule the interview.

You must be appropriately dressed for the interview – dress in a professional manner – a black or navy blue suit (with tie) is appropriate.

You shoes should be cleaned and polished to a shine.

Wear a belt at all times – the purpose of a belt is to hold your pants on your waist.

Your pants must cover, completely, your underwear – your underwear should never be seen.

It is indecent and inappropriate, to wear your pants below your buttocks at anytime, and even more so, for a job interview.

Do not wear a do-rag to an interview – it is out of place and inappropriate for a job interview.

First impressions are extremely important – the first time your prospective employer sees you, he should not be turned off by your appearance – do-rag, pants hanging below your butt. You will lose out – he or she will not employ you.

Your academic qualifications, will not be worth anything, if you appear for an interview in an unprofessional manner.

You must take all the documents requested for the interview – identification – resumé – social security card – passport – driver I.D., and whatever else you are asked to present, to the interviewer.

When you arrive for the interview, be sure to sign the visitor's log. The visitor's log is an Alibi. When you are ushered to the office, you must knock on the door before you enter (protocol). Give the interviewer, the appropriate greeting of the day, with a firm handshake, and eye-to-eye contact, wait for the invitation to sit.

You must maintain eye-to-eye contact during the interview, do not look down to the floor.

At the end of the interview, you should say, "Thank you," with a firm handshake and eye-to-eye contact.

You should know as much as possible about the Corporation you want to work for. If you want to work for McDonald's you should know the following –

1. When was McDonald's founded.
2. Who is the CEO.
3. Where is the home office.
4. The full menu served at McDonald's, and the prices of each.

5. You should know the requirements for owning your own McDonald's franchise.
6. Use the internet to obtain information you need, and as much as possible.

If you want to work for Black Enterprise Magazine, Newsweek, Times, Sports Illustrated, or any other organization, you must learn as much as possible about the organization.

Take the time to prepare for the interview – preparation is essential.

Do the research – be the best prepared interviewee.

"You Must Excel In Both Sports And Academics"

Many young men play football, basketball, baseball and other sports just for the fun of it.

Others play sports with a specific goal in mind – to go to college on an Athletic Scholarship, to be drafted by a Professional team, or to represent their country at International games, such as the Olympics, the World Games, or the Pan American Games.

To achieve these goals, a student athlete must be dedicated to his sport.

He has to get out of bed, for training, every morning, much earlier than most students. He or she has to run a few miles, lift weights, swim a few laps, and do whatever is necessary to get him or her into the physical and mental condition required to lay at the level of a Professional.

But, even more important, than any sport, is Academic Achievement. There is no guarantee, that any student athlete, regardless of how many records (athletic) he or she sets at the High school, College level, will be drafted by a Professional team – no guarantee whatsoever.

Therefore it is extremely important for you to excel on the Playing field, as well as on the Academic field.

There are two very important reasons for the student athlete with a Professional goal in mind to excel at both Academic and Athletic levels.

For example, should you receive a contract to play for a

Professional team, you must be able to sit with your Agent, or Attorneys, and read and fully understand what your interests are in that multi-million dollar contract.

If you can't read and understand your contract, you may be cheated of thousands of dollars, from what is promised in the contract .If you sign for $25 million dollars for 5 years, and a Stipulation that you must play every game of the season, or lose $3 million dollars, for every game missed, but you did not understand or even see the word "Stipulation", then you will legally lose $3 million dollars for each game missed regardless of the reason – injury, sickness, or death in the family.

You must know, and understand, what even a cell phone contract gives you.

The second reason is that if you are seriously injured, and unable to play the game again, especially if this injury occur early in your contract period, how would you earn money to support you and your family for the foreseeable future. Where will the money come from?

Are you qualified to work for a Corporation or can you start your own business, and work for yourself? Will you be forced to work for minimum wage?

You must excel on both fields – the Academic field, and the Athletic field.

"Ethics In The Workplace"

What is ethics? Ethics is "What is Right or Proper".

The right or proper thing to do – codes, standards, - sense of right and wrong.

When you are hired for a job, you are expected to follow all the Rules, Regulations, Laws, Procedures, and Protocols for that job – these are simple rules to follow, just different names. Any violation of the Rules can lead to a penalty – the penalty can be any of the following or a combination of –

1. Suspension – with or without pay.
2. Loss of pay.
3. Termination or loss of your job.
4. Demotion.
5. Loss of seniority.
6. Legal action against you.
7. Transfer to another location.
8. Counseling.

The basic rules for any job are as follows: -

1. Arrive on time.
2. Sign in, punch the clock (record your time of arrival – this is important for pay).
3. Be appropriately dressed – In uniform, or dress according to the dress code.
4. Always follows directions from your supervisor.

5. Be respectful to your supervisor.
6. Do not be afraid to ask questions, which will help you to perform your job well.
7. Avoid work-place confrontations – verbal or physical.
8. Always return to work on time,from your authorized break period – never exceed the time allotted for breaks.
9. Call ahead of time, at least one hour, if you know you are going to be late.
10. If the bus or train is late, write down the time, the train number or the bus number found on the sides of the train and bus.
11. Get a verification from the transit authority office or bus company, if the employer disputes your reason for arriving late.
12. Take advantage of classes or special training your job offers, or take classes at a college to learn more about your job and prepare yourself for any opportunities for promotion.
13. If you are asked to work extra hours,do not refuse, unless you have something very important to do. Don't just say "no."
    If asked to work overtime, you can say "I would like to, but I have to ....
    Most employers require documentation for unexcused or unexpected absences.

If you went to your doctor, or took your child or family member to the emergency room, get a note from your doctor, or a piece of document you received from the emergency room, such as a prescription as proof, or verification.

An employer hires a person because he has made the judgment that the new employee can perform the tasks assigned to him, in a professional manner, that would make his business successful.

If you fail, you will be fired – no businessman wants to lose money, which can lead to the failure of his business.

Therefore you must be an employee with "work ethics."

"It Is Disrespectful To Tease, Verbally Or Physically Abuse Anyone"

Do not abuse anyone who is Physically or Mentally Challenged. You might even be arrested for harassment, and it would be a legal matter if that person is physically harmed.

A physically challenged person is a person who uses a crutch, a cane, a walker, a wheel-chair, motorized or not, or cannot walk as a normal person walks because of an illness, accident, or birth defect.

A condition that occurs at birth is known as "congenital."

Many Physically and Mentally Challenged persons attained their condition at birth, due to a gene defect, or because of the abuse of either a legal or illegal drug by one or both parents, or because of an accident, such as a fall or auto-accident.

You should never disrespect a Physically or Mentally Challenged person, because you are also exposed to some of the same conditions that can make you Physically or Mentally Challenged - you can be struck by a bicycle or motor vehicle, be in a vehicle involved in a motor accident, fall on a sidewalk, fall down a stairway at home, or on the subway, and as a result sustain an injury to an arm, one or both legs, or a back injury, serious enough to cause temporary or permanent paralysis, of one or both legs, or one or both of your hands.

You must never disrespect anyone – young or old, fat or slim, tall or short, male or female, gay or heterosexual, mentally or physically challenged, different nationality, style of dress ,someone of a different religion, or for any other reason.

We are all human beings – the blood in everybody is of the same color, red. Blood from a man in India or China can be used to save a person in Africa. Blood from a Caucasian (white) man can be used to save the life of an African American, and so can the blood from an African American man, save the life of a Caucasian (white) man.

We are all human beings regardless of how much or little we possess – where we live – the clothes we wear, designer or not – what car we drive – what sneaker we wear – what God we worship, or what foods we eat.

We are all human beings, but different in many ways.

We are all like cars – different shape, sizes, and models.

Teasing, bullying, verbally abusing or physically abusing, or laughing at a person, because he or she walks with a limp or artificial leg, should never be a source of fun for you. It is never fun. What can prevent you from losing one or both legs today, or sometime in the future? No one knows.

It is a lack of respect to laugh at someone because he or she is different from you – you are behaving in a disrespectful manner, and inflicting emotional pain on that person.

Stop – do not engage in, or participate in actions that are hurtful to others.

If your friends are engaged in such behavior, tell them they are wrong, and tell them, "it is not right to disrespect a person, because he or she is different."

Stop reading this page, right now – close your eyes – can you imagine someone abusing you, teasing you, laughing at you, can you hear the laughter – can you see your mother in a wheelchair, her leg broken due to a fall, and being pushed in circles by a bully. Would you accept that?

Always observe the Golden Rule – "Do unto others, as you would like them to do to you."

"Do Not Bully"

What is a bully? – A bully is all of the following –

1. A bully is a pest.
2. A bully torments another person.
3. A bully is a tease.
4. A bully harasses another person.
5. A bully persecutes another person.
6. A bully is one who is threatening to others.
7. A bully bullies someone, whom he believes is weak.

A bully targets the following persons –

1. One who is overweight.
2. A new kid on the block.
3. A person from another country.
4. A person who dresses differently because of his culture.
5. A new kid at school.
6. A kid who has more money, than others, to spend.
7. A kid who speaks with a different accent – he may be from another part of the country, or a foreign country.
8. A kid who is an "A" student.

Bullying is wrong – you are also different from other people in several ways also, but no one is attacking you.

Would you be happy if someone were to kick, push, spit on you, or call you ugly names, because you are different, or appear to be weak?

Bullying is not only a physical attack on a person bullying is done on the internet – it is called cyber-bullying.

Do not use the internet, to harass, threaten, spread gossip, call a person ugly names, or spread false stories about a person – this is cyber-bullying.

There are serious consequences bullying carries.

There are serious consequences for the bully, and the person who is being bullied. If you are caught, you will face the penalties the Laws of your State provide for bullies. You can spend some time in jail.

The person who is being bullied, becomes fearful, whenever he or she has to leave the safety of home, and may feign sickness, just to stay home, to get away from the bully.

When a student stays away from school, because of a bully, he or she is denied the opportunity to an education. This is a violation of that student's rights, and you the bully, are responsible – you are denying the student his right to go to school – you are the one who is preventing that child from going to school.

The person who is bullied on the internet, is terrified, because someone he does not know, or has never seen, is threatening him, calling him names, insults him, taunts him, and is spreading unflattering stories about him or her.

He feels as if he is being haunted by a ghost – he feels helpless – he is unhappy – and is always fearful that someday, someone will do him harm.

Several kids have killed themselves because they were bullied. When a person kills himself – that person has committed suicide. Suicide is one of the most serious consequences of bullying.

Would you like to be the person, who is responsible for a kid who killed himself, because you bullied him from day to day. If you should ever be that person that caused a child to kill himself ,because you bullied him, you will certainly be put behind bars.

If any of your friends are bullies, do not take part, or encourage them, by standing, and have good laugh. Bullying is not fun.

Tell your friends that, "it is wrong, it is not right, stop that now." Tell an adult about it – tell your teacher – tell your parents.

Tell the school crossing guard. Do something about it. Take action against the bullying you witness everyday. Do not stay silent.

Someone can be seriously hurt – someone can take their own life – someone can commit suicide – someone can be dead.

You are not a "snitch," because you spoke out against bullying.

You are a responsible person whenever you speak out against anything that is wrong.

When you speak out against bullying, you could be saving someone from Mental and Physical Abuse, or you could be saving someone from Committing Suicide.

If you are being bullied, either in person or on the internet, you should always tell an adult about it. Do not keep it a secret. You must report bullying when it occurs, so that the bully can be caught, stopped, and punished to the fullest extent of the Law.

Bullying can be observed in a range of behaviors. You are a bully if you engage in any of the following –

1. Name calling – social exclusion – teasing – threats – ganging up on another child – fist fights – kicking – punching or hitting in the back, taking away ones money or toy – pushing - spitting on another person, or hitting another child, because he refuses your challenge to fight him.

Are you a bully? Are you being bullied?

"Common Everyday Etiquettes"

It is polite to offer the greetings of the day to a passerby, your neighbor, your teacher, your friends, when you meet in school, or on your way to school, and last but not least.our Senior Citizens, or the elderly. "Good morning, how are you today?" is an appropriate way to greet someone.

It is polite to say "Thank You" or "Thank You Very Much," to someone who has just provided you with a service – the bus driver – the taxi driver – a sales person – the cashier – the mail person – the nurse (school)- the janitor – your teacher at the end of a class or a private consultation.

It is polite to say "Thank You," when someone responds to your request for a pencil, a glass of water, directions to a certain place, or any request for some form of assistance.

You are expected to say "Please" and "Thank You" at home, so you should display those same etiquettes when you are away from home.

You should say, "I am sorry," or "Excuse me," when you step on someone's toes, or rub against them in small spaces, such as on a bus or train, and other public places, for example, a restaurant, a Library, or in a waiting line, or other crowded environment.

It is considered rude and inconsiderate to play loud music on the bus, train and other places, for example, a restaurant, the Library, and when in the classroom or hallway.

You should use earphones for your private listening pleasure only, and do not disturb the person, or persons sitting or standing next to you. If the person next to you, can hear the music from your earphones or headpiece, then your earphones or headpiece are defective.

Always carry a handkerchief with you, to cover your nose and mouth when you sneeze or cough, or to wipe away perspiration from your face on a hot humid day.

Never jump ahead of your position, when on a waiting line in the supermarket – the bus stop – a cashier's line – at the movies while waiting to purchase tickets – or for any other purpose where a waiting line is necessary.

Always wait your turn. Never jump ahead of a Senior Citizen because you think of them as "weak or slow" – doing so is disrespectful to anyone, regardless of age, sex, race, or build or height.

Do not litter – it is both untidy and unlawful.

Always pay your fare on the train, bus, or taxi. The failure to pay your fare, or "fare evasion," is unlawful.

You could be arrested, and face the penalty of paying a fine, to the Courts, of hundreds of dollars.

Always offer your seat to a Senior Citizen, a female, or a physically challenged person, when you are on a bus or train.

Always offer your set to a pregnant woman, or to a woman with a baby or child in her arms.

Always offer your seat to a father, who has a baby or small child in his arms.

You should also consider offering your seat to anyone with a small child in tow when you are on the bus or train.

"What To Do With An Unplanned or Unwanted Pregnancy"

A) Do not deny it – admit to it, if you are certain that you are the father of the unborn child – if you are not certain it is you who impregnated that female, do a paternity test, to determine whether or not you are the father.
B) If you are the father, do not run and hide – it is the father and mother, who must care for the baby – it is your responsibility to assist the mother, at all times.
C) Inform your parents – do not allow anyone else to tell your parents you are a father before you do – it is an act of respect to inform them before anyone else does.
   Do not hide the pregnancy from your parents. Your parents and the girls parents must be told of the pregnancy.
D) If your relationship with your parents is not an amicable one, or your parents are very strict, or have deep religious convictions, tell someone else.

Tell an elder brother or sister, an uncle or an aunt, your pastor, or someone else at church, who can help you, by telling you what to do, where to go to prepare for the arrival of the new baby.

Young man, you must be responsible for your actions – stand up and say, "That child is mine," say it again, "That child is mine" – do not abandon your new family –

You and your child's mother are now new parents, first time parents,

As new parents, you will need lots of help – financial, babysitting assistance, since both of you are still in school, parenting instruction, family planning, and much more.

Therefore it is very important whenever a pregnancy happens, both sets of parents must be notified, so that all preparations are made for the arrival of the new baby.

The most important of the preparations, is the health of the mother during the nine months she is bearing the baby in her womb.

The mother must eat healthy – eat the appropriate foods, so that both she and the unborn child, are in the best of health – regular prenatal clinic visits must be made – see the doctor on a regular basis – never miss scheduled clinic appointments.

It is important for the mother and the unborn child to be in good health, up to the day of birth and after birth and beyond.

It is the responsibility of every parent, to feed, clothe, protect, and educate their children.

If a child is found to be in poor care, the parents can be reported to the Children Welfare Agencies, who will in most cases, remove the child or children from the parents care, and give that responsibility to a Foster parent.

Children already in Foster care, can also be taken away from that Foster parent(s) and placed with another Foster parent for better care.

In certain cases the Child Welfare Agency has charged parents with child neglect, endangering the welfare of a minor, or child abuse. The child or children in these cases are placed under the Jurisdiction of the Courts, which appoint Law Guardians to oversee the welfare of the children.

When a young man impregnates a young woman, he is automatically starting a new family.

A man with a family has tremendous responsibilities. He must take care of his family – provide food – provide shelter – provide protection – provide education for his children.

He was to provide for the needs of his children until they reach the age of eighteen, when they are considered adults, and can make decisions independent of their parents approval.

But the parents responsibilities do not end at the age of eighteen.

The next phase of the children's lives is a College Education. Unless the parents have a college fund or some other source of money to finance their children's College Education, they will have to work extra hours, or take a bank loan, in addition to Student Loans or Grants to pay for collect costs.

Therefore it is appropriate and wise for a young man to be fully prepared to start a family.

How does one prepare to start a family?

The very first and most important step is – do not have any babies – and how do you do that – stay away from sexual activity – do not have sex – abstain.

Young boys (and girls) must not engage in premarital sex – no sex before you and the girl are married.

The next stop, and a very important step it is – Complete Your Education – all the way through College. – earn a Degree.

You and your wife will need to earn a good salary to provide the necessities for your new family – food, clothes, rent, transportation money, babysitting, education for your child from Kindergarten through College, medication, utilities – light and gas, and many more until your child or children leave home to be on their own.

A good education qualifies you to earn a higher salary than someone with a high school diploma or no high school diploma – the higher the salary, the more and better things you can afford to buy.

A young man who is still in school and with no sources of income cannot adequately raise a family – preparation to raise a family is the smart and wise thing to do.

A pregnancy that was not planned interrupts the education of both the mother and father. Both of them may have to leave school, to take care of the new baby, and may not, for whatever reason, return to school to complete their education.

Without an education, it is definitely difficult to raise a family, because your ability to earn a good salary is thwarted by the lack of a good education – this makes it difficult to acquire many of the things you would like to have or do, such as going to the movies, or on a vacation, buying your child a toy he or she wants, or some new clothes for you and your wife. *See trade section.

Overall, you must have a plan – Family Planning – to raise a family, after you and the young lady decide on a life together. Among the many things to consider when planning to start a family are the health of both of you, how many children you would like to have, one or ten, where would you like to live, do you want to rent an apartment, or buy a house, how would the bills be paid, should both husband and wife work, do you want to own one car or two cars, how would you and your wife pay for your child's or children's education, would you need babysitting, would either of you want to further your education, would both of you, or one of you need to have a second job, or overtime to meet the expenses.

There are many more things to consider – you should consult with your parents, pastor, elder brother, or any organization that helps couples plan the starting and raising of a family.

Preparation is essential.

If a young boy impregnates a young woman, he should immediately inform both parents his and hers.

It is the respectable and responsible thing to do.

Everyone – you, your child's mother, and the parents of both of you, should sit together, to discuss the care of the newborn baby.

As first time parents, you will need all the help and advice you can get.

Do you want to care for the child with the help of its grandparents or do you want to give up the child for Foster care.

Foster care is care by a total stranger, but care given by a family member or relative is known as Guardianship.

Do not ever abandon a baby – in a garbage can, on a park bench – at the foot of a tree, in the toilet bowl, or anywhere else you may think of.

If the arrival of a newborn baby leaves you scared, confused, troubled or at a loss, do not abandon that child – act in a Responsible and Humane way – take the baby to a Police Precinct – a Hospital – a Church – a Doctor's Office, or to anyone who will assist you.

It is your Utmost Responsibility to give your Newborn Baby to someone who will take care of it. If You Do Not Want The Child – Do not Abandon Your Child.

"Consider The Earning Possibilities Of A Trade"

There are Alternatives to a College Education, if one does not have the financial resources to go to College, or for other reasons College is not an option.

Electricians, plumbers ,carpenters, known as the Construction Trades, welders, auto body repair, automotive services and repair, and air conditioning ,are Professions considered not prestigious or glamorous, as Doctors or Professional athletes.

These Professions or Trades, as they are called, do pay high salaries, much more than the minimum wage. The Trades provide the freedom to decide one's own work schedule and job security, especially if one is the owner of the business.

A person who owns a business, is the boss and supervisor of that business. He or she can make as much money as he desires. No one is in a position to tell him he is worth $8.00 or "20.00 or more or less for his service. He, the business owner, decides for himself, how many hours a day he wants to work, how many days of the week, or how many months of the year he wants to work.

He can decide if he wants to work during the spring and summer months, when the weather is warmer, or work during the winter months and take off summer months to spend time with his family.

Auto body repair provides the opportunity for High Earnings. There are always cars and other vehicles to be repaired, because auto accidents happen all day, everyday, across the Cities, States, and Country.

Doors, fenders, bumpers, trunks, hoods, wheels and other parts of vehicles can be damaged in an accident. One can earn fifty ($50.00) dollars and more, just to fix a door – fix two (2) doors in a day and you can earn $100-$200 just for one day.

An employee who earns $8.00 an hour, needs to work at least three (3) days to earn $200.00

An electrician can earn about $70.00 to fix a malfunctioning light switch or $120.00 to install new electrical wiring.

He can also earn $60-$80 to repair a boiler that heats a home. An auto body paint job can pay as much as $600-$1,000 a week, or more. An engine that needs repair, especially if it must be removed from the car to effect repairs, can pay $800 or more, depending on the extent of the repairs to be made.

A plumber who is hired to fix a leaky faucet, can earn $50-$150, or more, depending on the size of the leak and where it is located. If the pipe is located in the ceiling, or the wall, it may be necessary for the plumber to cut out a portion of the wall or ceiling to reach the leaky pipe.

He is now doing the job of a carpenter and plumber, to repair the leaky pipe. The extra work increases the cost of the repair to the pipe or faucet.

You can work for both a plumbing company, and for yourself in your spare time, thus earning two salaries.

The money you earn as a plumber, electrician, auto mechanic, or other trade can be used to supplement your tuition and other college costs. If you decide not to go to college, the Trades can pay you Excellent Wages – you can work both for Yourself and Someone else. Work Full time for your employer, and Part time for yourself.

Plan to open your Own Business, Investigate what you need to do to Open Your Own Business.

At the conclusion of training in one of the Trades, you would need to gain some Experience, to be hired, and paid the wages of one who has Considerable Experience.

To gain that experience, you may have to work for a much lower wage. or volunteer your services, until you acquire the necessary experience to achieve your goals. You must make sacrifices – lower wage,or no wage, until you gain the amount of experience required to be hired with full wages.

For example, if you choose auto body repair, the auto body repair shop owner, may not start training you immediately. He may ask you to run errands, such as purchasing auto body parts, or paints. He may assign you the task of doing inventory once a week, he may ask you to clean the tools at the end of the day, or sweep the floors.

These tasks are necessary for the efficient operation of the business.

Your willingness to assist in the other aspects of the business, other than just auto body repairs, will determine whether or not the owner of that auto body repair business will hire you.

The simple task of sweeping the floor can be the deciding factor in the businessman's decision to hire or not to hire you.

It is therefore very important for you to have an excellent work relationship, either as a volunteer or paid employee with your employer.

Your work history must be impeccable – do all that is required of you to reach your goals. Sometimes more may be required of you. Just do it.

You must creep before you walk.

"Continuing Education"

Learning does not end when you receive a High School Diploma,, or a College Degree.

Life itself is a school. One can learn something everyday. Keep your eyes and ears open – look – listen – observe, and ask questions.

Seek to learn more about something that grabs your attention. Use the Library as one of the main sources of information. You must read – read – read.

Reading is essential.

Use these sources for the information you seek – the Library – Google – space.com – live science.com – NASA.TV. – National Geographic – Museums – Archives – Historical Societies – grandfather – grandmother – aunts- uncles – teachers – other sources.

Many of the websites will direct you to other sources of information about what you are looking for, and as you search, your interests will expand.

The following topics are suggested for your continuing education

I. Historical Events

A) The first airplane flight
B) The first space-craft.
C) The first manned space flight.
D) The first manned moon landing.
E) The first heart operation

F) The first heart transplant.
G) The first separation of Siamese Twin babies.
H) The use of the first Atomic Bomb.
I) The first Super Sonic JET Aircraft – The first JET Aircraft.
J) The first Space Vehicle to return from space and land like an airplane.
K) The first Woman in space – The first African American Woman in space.
L) The Assassinations of President John Kennedy and his brother, Attorney General Robert Kennedy.
M) The Assassination of Civil Rights Leader, Dr. Martin Luther King and the Assassination of Malcolm X.
N) The explosion of Space Shuttles in flight.
O) The first Bullet Train (high speed).
P) The first Palm Size telephone (cell phone).
Q) The first African American Male to run for President.
R) The first African American Female to run for President.

II. Entertainment –

A) Louis Armstrong
B) Harry Belafonte
C) Billie Holliday
D) Leontyne Price
E) Aretha Franklin
F) Ella Fitzgerald
G) Irvin Berlin
H) Scott Joplin
I) Frank Sinatra
J) Bing Crosby
K) Sammy Davis, Jr.
L) Alvin Ailey
M) Bill Cosby
N) Ray Charles
O) Burl Ives

P) Nat King Cole
Q) Tony Bennett
R) Al Martino
S) Dean Martin
T) Lisa Minelli – Judy Garland

Comedians, Comediennes

Phyllis Diller
George Carlin
Richard Pryor
Milton Berle
Carol Burnett
Eddie Murphy
Redd Fox
Johnny Carson
Bob Hope
John Belushi
Lucille Ball (Lucy)
Flip Wilson
Gilda Radner
Joey Bishop

These personalities are only a few of many.

The Military –

1. General George Marshall
2. General George Patton
3. General William Westmoreland
4. General Schwartzkoff
5. General Colin Powell
6. General Chappie James Jr.
7. General Omar Bradley

Internationally known leaders

1. Nelson Mandela
2. Mahatma Gandhi
3. Dr. Martin Luther King, Jr.

4. Kwame Nkrumah

Internationally known Female Heads of State –

1. Margaret Thatcher
2. Golda Meir
3. Indira Gandhi
4. Chandrika Bandarnike
5. Portia Simpson
6. Eugena Charles
7. Angela Merkel

Jesse Jackson
Barack Obama
Shirley Chisolm
Senator Carol Mosley Braun
Governor David Wilder
Governor David Patterson
Malcolm X
Stokely Carmichael
Angela Davis
Thurgood Marshall
Clarence Thomas

Dr. Ben Carson
Henry Ford
Garrett Morgan
Charles Drew
Granville T. Woods
Jesse Eugene Russell
The Rockerfeller Family
The Vanderbilt Family
George Washington Carver

All weather tires

The Korean War
World War I – World War II
The Vietnam Conflict
Iraq War
Afghanistan War

Rosa Parks
Harriet Tubman
Fannie Lou Hamer
Sojourner Truth

Frances Gary Powers
Ronald McNair
Dr. Mae Jamison

Ralph Bunch
John Kennedy
Carol Simpson

Ed Bradley
Robert Kennedy
Walter Kronkite

Colonel Charles Bolden
John Glen
Christie McCauliffe
Amelia Earhart
Bessie Smith
The Wright Brothers

Charlaine Hunter Gault
Oprah Winfrey
John Hope Franklin
Professor Louis Gates

Marva Colins

Sports figures –

Babe Ruth – Jackie Robinson – Curt Flood – Hank Aaron
Joe Louis – Jack Johnson – Muhammad Ali – Jake LaMotta
Bill Russel – Bruce Jenner - Jessie Owens – Rocky Marciano
Althea Gibson – Billie Jean King – Arthur Ashe – Joe Frazier – Wilma Rudolph – Sisters Serina and Venus Williams.

About the Author

The Author is a father of five children, and grandfather of four. He is a former School Teacher, and a retired STAFF SERGEANT IN THE UNITED STATES ARMY.

He has served his community in many areas, including mentoring,educational and recreational activities for young people.

TO MY SON ARSENIO, MY GREATEST MOTIVATOR, JANET,
AND DONNA MY MOST ARDENT SUPPORTER.

www.ingramcontent.com/pod-product-compliance
Ingram Content Group UK Ltd.
Pitfield, Milton Keynes, MK11 3LW, UK
UKHW041938190726
13854UKWH00004B/1655